Three

Ben Brown was born in London in 1969. His plays
include *Four Letter Word* (Edinburgh Fringe), Cameron
Mackintosh New Writing Award 1994; *All Things
Considered* (Stephen Joseph Theatre, Hampstead
Theatre, Petit Théâtre de Paris, Marian Street Theatre,
Sydney, Zimmertheater, Heidelberg), nominated for a
Writers' Guild Best Play Award and the TMA Best New
Play Award 1997; *Larkin With Women* (Stephen Joseph
Theatre, West Yorkshire Playhouse, Coventry Belgrade,
Manchester Library Theatre, Orange Tree Theatre
2006), Express Play of the Year, TMA Best New Play
2000; and *The Promise* (Orange Tree Theatre, 2010).

BEN BROWN

Three Days in May

faber and faber

First published in 2011
by Faber and Faber Limited
74–77 Great Russell Street, London WC1B 3DA

Typeset by Country Setting, Kingsdown, Kent CT14 8ES
Printed and bound by CPI Group (UK) Ltd, Croydon, CR0 4YY

A CIP record for this book
is available from the British Library

ISBN 978–0–571–28299–9

2 4 6 8 10 9 7 5 3 1

Three Days in May was produced by Bill Kenwright and first performed at the Theatre Royal, Windsor, on 16 August 2011. The cast was as follows:

Winston Churchill Warren Clarke
Neville Chamberlain Michael Sheldon
Lord Halifax Jeremy Clyde
Jock Colville James Alper
Arthur Greenwood Dicken Ashworth
Paul Reynaud Timothy Kightley
General Dill Paul Ridley
Clement Attlee Ben Farrow

Director Alan Strachan
Designer Gary McCann
Lighting Designer Mark Howett
Sound Designer Martin Hodgson

Characters

Winston Churchill

Neville Chamberlain

Lord Halifax

Clement Attlee

Arthur Greenwood

Jock Colville

Paul Reynaud

General Dill

For Jenny

With thanks to Bill and Alan

THREE DAYS IN MAY

'It is where the balance quivers,
and the proportions are veiled in mist,
that the opportunity for world-saving
decisions presents itself.'

Winston S. Churchill, *The Gathering Storm*

Act One

PROLOGUE

Sunday, the 26 May 1940.
Morning.
As the house lights come down, the sombre sound of a church bell tolling out the time. It rings ten times as the lights come up on five dark-suited men kneeling in prayer at the front of the stage facing the audience.
Pause.
The last chime fades out as a good-looking young man (twenty-five) with greased-back hair and wearing a suit and tie, walks on to the stage and faces the audience.

Jock Hello. My name's Jock Colville and I'm dead now.

Beat.

But this isn't my funeral. This is the service held at Westminster Abbey on Sunday 26th May 1940. The National Day of Prayer.

Beat.

And that's the British War Cabinet. On its knees.

He turns to face them.

There's Churchill, of course, in the middle. My boss. Well, everyone's boss, I suppose . . .

He looks at Churchill, sixty-five and jowly.

And there to the right of him is my old boss, Neville Chamberlain . . .

He looks at Chamberlain, seventy-one, with a moustache and greying hair.

3

Prime Minister until just sixteen days ago, he is still, people forget, in the Cabinet and still Leader of the Conservative Party in the new coalition government.

He looks again at the ill-looking and depressed Chamberlain.

To the right of Chamberlain, naturally, is Chamberlain's right-hand man, Lord Halifax.

He looks at Halifax, fifty-nine, tall and willowy.

Still Foreign Secretary, he is known as the Holy Fox for his love of the High Church and hunting . . . Maybe this was his idea?

Halifax lifts his head and speaks.

Halifax Prayer is the one instrument which even the humblest amongst us can use in his country's service.

Then lowers it again.
Jock smiles.

Jock Finally, to the left of Churchill, are the two new-boy Labour Ministers. Clement Attlee, my future boss after the war . . .

He looks at Attlee, fifty-seven and balding, with a dark moustache.

Who Churchill once described as a modest little man with plenty to be modest about . . .

Attlee lifts his head and smiles but says nothing. Then lowers it again.

And on the far left, his deputy, Arthur Greenwood. A Yorkshireman.

He looks at Greenwood, sixty, with small round glasses, who lifts his head.

Greenwood Labour hates war, but it hates Fascism even more.

4

Jock smiles as Greenwood lowers his head.
Then turns back to the audience.

Jock So there they are. The five men whose job it is somehow to extricate the country from its worst crisis in nearly a thousand years . . . as Hitler has just swept through Western Europe in little over a fortnight and now occupies Austria, Czechoslovakia, Poland, Norway, Denmark and Holland, and is on the point of conquering Belgium and France. Moreover, he has a non-aggression pact with Stalin's Russia, Mussolini's Fascist Italy seems about to come in on Germany's side and America, still in the grip of its isolationists, is nowhere to be seen . . . Meanwhile, almost half a million British and French troops are surrounded in northern France and appear to be entirely at Hitler's mercy.

He glances at the kneeling men.

So you can see why they're praying.

Beat.

This is what Chamberlain wrote in his diary that night.

Chamberlain raises his head.

Chamberlain The blackest day of all . . . I could hardly attend to the service with this load on my mind . . . A terrible position for France and ourselves. The most horrible in our history.

He lowers it again.

Jock Now I'm sure you know about Dunkirk and how, in the days after this one, the British Army escaped by the skin of its teeth from the Germans at the start of the war. But what you may not know is that at precisely the same time back in London, the War Cabinet were seriously considering throwing in the towel and suing for peace. And the reason you don't is because Churchill didn't want you to. He didn't want people to think there was ever a moment when Britain wobbled. When even he wobbled . . . for a moment.

He looks at Churchill still kneeling in prayer.

But after all this time . . . well, I think it's all right to tell you now.

He smiles.

So to go back to the beginning, our story starts on that fateful last Sunday morning in May when practically everyone but me was at the Abbey and a telegram came through from Paris saying that the French Prime Minister, Monsieur Reynaud, was flying in and wished to see the Prime Minister immediately . . . and alone.

Beat.

Needless to say, it was raining.

The sound of rain as the lights cross-fade from Westminster Abbey to the Cabinet room.

SCENE ONE

The Cabinet Room, 10 Downing Street, London.
Sunday, the 26 May.
The large Cabinet table with chairs round it dominates the room, and set apart from it downstage right is a small desk (Jock's) with a chair facing sideways to the audience. Upstage of that is a bookcase.
The sound of rain continues.
Paul Reynaud – sixty-one, small and dark – waits alone, looking anxious and shaken.
He glances at his watch impatiently.
Then Jock enters through a door stage left.
Reynaud turns round quickly but is disappointed when he sees it's only Jock.

Jock smiles apologetically.

Jock He's got the message and is on his way.

Reynaud Good.

But Reynaud still looks full of concern.
Jock wonders what to do next.

Jock Um . . . *Voulez-vous . . . avoir . . . quelque chose . . . à boire?*

Reynaud looks at him for a moment, unimpressed.

Café, peut-être?

Reynaud No, thank you. Not until the Prime Minister arrives.

Jock smiles.

Jock Right. Of course.

Pause.
Jock continues to stand around awkwardly.

Shouldn't be long.

Reynaud glances at him and Jock smiles weakly back.

It's not far from here. The Abbey.

Reynaud Mm . . .

Jock thinks desperately.

Jock Just a few minutes' walk, in fact.

Beat.

Down the road, turn right and across Parliament Square –

Reynaud Yes, I know where it is.

Jock Yes, of course. Sorry.

Beat.

Reynaud Look, haven't you got some work to do?

Jock Well, yes, but –

Reynaud Then please, feel free to get on with it.

Jock Yes, of course. Thank you.

Feeling he has done his duty, Jock goes to his desk upstage and begins sorting through the red Prime Ministerial box.

Reynaud continues to wait anxiously.

Then finally the door opens and Churchill enters carrying his gas mask.

Reynaud Prime Minister . . .

Reynaud moves towards him.

Churchill Premier . . .

They shake hands and look at it each other for a moment.

Good to see you.

Reynaud And you, Prime Minister. And you.

They break and Churchill puts his gas mask down.

Churchill But you haven't got a drink. Jock, why haven't you given Monsieur Reynaud a drink?

Jock Well, I . . .

Churchill What would you like, Premier?

Reynaud Perhaps a little cognac.

Churchill Of course. Jock, two cognacs.

Jock Yes, sir.

Jock pours the drinks.

Churchill Sorry I wasn't here to meet you. How was your flight?

Reynaud Well, I wasn't shot down. And in these times we must be grateful for that, *non?*

Churchill looks at him uncertainly.

Churchill Mm . . .

Jock arrives with the drinks, giving one to Reynaud first.

Reynaud Thank you.

And then to Churchill.
Churchill raises his glass.

Churchill To the Alliance.

Reynaud hesitates before lifting his glass.

Reynaud Yes . . . the Alliance.

They drink.

So . . . you may be wondering why I have come all this way to see you, instead of just picking up the telephone.

Churchill It did cross my mind.

Reynaud Well then, I shall get straight to the point.

Beat.

We received news last night from our Ambassador in Rome that Mussolini is about to enter the war.

Churchill takes this in.

Churchill Yes, well, that doesn't altogether surprise me.

Reynaud No . . . But for us I fear it could be the last straw. You see, as it is, we have only fifty divisions left to face Germany's one hundred and fifty, and if Italy comes in we will not be able to add the ten that are currently stationed on our south-east border.

Churchill Yes, I see that. But once our counter-attack starts, then we will have the Germans on the back foot for a change and everything may turn around. So, if General Weygand would just give the order, Lord Gort will attack too and then they can link up north of the Somme and –

Reynaud There will be no counter-attack.

Churchill is stunned.

Churchill What?

Reynaud General Weygand says it is impossible. The Germans are too strong for us.

Churchill takes this in.

Churchill But if we don't try, how can we know that?

Reynaud Oh, we have tried, Prime Minister. God knows we have. But we have no answer to their tanks and aircraft. Without more air cover ourselves, that is. And of course that depends on you.

Churchill looks uncomfortable.

Churchill Yes, well . . . we have already sent a quarter of our fighters and lost them all. And you will understand that we must hold back some for our own defence.

Reynaud Oh yes, I understand. After all, we must all look for our own salvation, *non?*

He looks at Churchill.

Which is why France must now look elsewhere for hers.

He drinks.

Churchill What do you mean?

Beat.

Reynaud Our Ambassador says we may be able to prevent Italy coming in if we are prepared to pay a certain price.

Churchill Meaning?

Reynaud France must give up Corsica, Tunisia and Algeria – and Britain, Gibraltar, Malta and Suez.

Churchill . . . Suez?

Reynaud Yes. Mussolini again stressed the humiliation he feels at the presence of the British at both gates of the Mediterranean . . . But in return for these, he might be persuaded not only to stay out of the war but, perhaps more importantly, to play the role of mediator for a wider European settlement.

Churchill reacts.

Churchill As he did at Munich, you mean?

Reynaud . . . Yes.

Churchill How kind of him.

A thought suddenly occurs to him.

Have you been offered peace terms by Germany, then?

Reynaud No . . . not yet. But we know that we can get an offer if we want one.

Churchill Yes, I dare say you can.

Reynaud reacts uncomfortably.

Reynaud Look, we are prepared to fight on. Of course we are. But the truth is France cannot resist for much longer . . . So, I think we have no choice but to make an approach to Italy, both to try and keep her out of the war, and to . . . mediate a wider European settlement.

Churchill You mean sue for peace.

Reynaud hesitates.

Reynaud Regrettably . . . yes.

A solemn pause.

But of course we shall do nothing without your agreement.

Churchill Of course.

Churchill looks at him penetratingly.
Reynaud gives a little smile. Then looks away.

And you absolutely refuse to counter-attack?

Reynaud . . . I'm afraid so, yes. I would like to, of course, but General Weygand assures me it would have no chance of success.

Churchill thinks.

Churchill Very well then. I shall put your suggestion to my colleagues.

Reynaud Thank you.

Reynaud is relieved.

And if I may say so, I feel sure that Mr Chamberlain and Lord Halifax will receive it with sympathy and understanding.

Churchill Mm . . .

Churchill reflects on this with concern.

In the meantime, though, since you have no intention of attacking, I trust General Weygand will issue an order to Lord Gort for the British Expeditionary Force to fall back on the coast?

Reynaud Of course.

Churchill Thank you.

They get up.

Reynaud I shall wait to hear from you then.

Churchill Yes.

They look at each other for a moment with sadness.

Reynaud Well . . . till we meet again.

Churchill Yes . . . *Au revoir*, Premier.

They shake hands, knowing it might be for the last time.
Then Reynaud goes.
Churchill thinks for a moment.
Then turns to Jock.

Summon the War Cabinet for an urgent meeting at two p.m.

Jock Yes, sir.

Jock goes out.
Churchill is left alone.
He stands there for a moment.
Then collapses into his chair and puts his head in his hands as the lights fade.

SCENE TWO

Sunday afternoon.
The War Cabinet is in progress.
Jock sits at his desk taking minutes.

Churchill So there you have it, gentlemen. The French army, the rock upon which all our hopes have been built these last few years, has simply disintegrated, and they now wish to sue for peace.

Pause.

Halifax Yes, well, that is indeed a dark picture you have painted for us, Prime Minister . . . a very dark picture.

The others nod.

Churchill Of course, if we could only send more fighters, then perhaps –

Chamberlain Well, we can't.

Halifax No.

Greenwood and Attlee shake their heads too.

Chamberlain The Air Ministry have made it clear that we already have the absolute minimum left to defend ourselves. And perhaps not even that.

Halifax nods.

Churchill Yes, so everyone keeps telling me.

Beat.

Halifax So, much though one hates to say it, I really can't see that we have any alternative but to go along with the French approach to Italy . . .

Chamberlain No . . .

Churchill, Attlee and Greenwood look unhappy but no one can gainsay him.

Halifax But amongst all the darkness, perhaps there is one ray of light, as surely the last thing Signor Mussolini wants is to see Herr Hitler dominating all Europe. In which case, surely, he will be anxious, if he can, to persuade him to take a more reasonable attitude.

Chamberlain nods in agreement.

Chamberlain Yes, well, one would certainly hope so.

Attlee nods and 'Mm's too.
Pause.

Churchill But it doesn't seem right . . .

Halifax looks confused.

Halifax Right?

Churchill No.

Halifax Well, indeed. But, alas, the Kingdom of God and the Kingdom of the World are very different places.

Churchill No, I mean we are in a different position from France and we must remember that.

Halifax Ah . . .

Churchill thinks.

Churchill We still have powers of resistance – and attack – which the French do not . . . And they are likely to be offered decent terms, which we should not, since Hitler is intent on destroying our Empire . . . So perhaps if France cannot defend herself, it is *better* that she should get out of the war rather than drag us into a settlement which involves intolerable terms? . . . And there is no limit to the terms which Germany will impose upon us if she has her way. So from that point of view, I would *rather* France was out of the war before she was broken up, so that she could retain the position of a strong neutral whose factories cannot be used against us.

Attlee But if France goes out of the war now, Herr Hitler will be able to turn on us the sooner.

Greenwood That's true.

Chamberlain Yes . . .

Halifax nods.

Churchill Yes, well . . . of course I hope that France will hang on . . . But at the same time we must be careful not to be forced into the weak position in which we simply go to Signor Mussolini and invite him to ask Herr Hitler to treat us nicely.

Pause as they all see that this is indeed what is being suggested.

Halifax I don't disagree with you, Prime Minister. But I attach perhaps rather more importance than you to the desirability of allowing France to at least . . . try out the possibilities of European equilibrium.

He pauses.

So I think we might accede to Monsieur Reynaud's request whilst emphasising of course that if there is any suggestion of terms which affect our independence, we should not look at them for a moment.

Beat.

Or at any rate I can see no harm in trying this line of approach.

He looks to Chamberlain for support.

Churchill Mr Chamberlain?

Chamberlain Yes, well, I must say I tend to agree with the Foreign Secretary.

Halifax is pleased.

So rather than saying to Mussolini, as the French want us to, that we are prepared to do a deal with him in regard to certain *named* places, we – or the French – could simply say to him that he must consider the future of Europe, including his own future. And that if he is prepared to collaborate with us in getting tolerable terms, then we will be prepared to discuss Italian demands with him.

Halifax Exactly.

Churchill thinks.

Now, of course, nobody wants to give up a jot of our Empire, but we must face the fact that it is now, alas, not so much a question of imposing a complete defeat upon Germany as of . . . well, safeguarding our independence.

Chamberlain Yes . . .

Halifax glances at Chamberlain.
Everyone looks to Churchill.
Pause.

Churchill (*reluctantly*) Yes, well . . . I suppose right now I should be thankful if we could get out of this jam just by giving up a little territory . . . Malta, Gibraltar . . . perhaps some African colonies . . .

The others are surprised. They have never heard him talk like this before.
He looks up and sees them looking at him.

But I don't think we are likely to be offered such terms.

Halifax Well, that remains to be seen. But, as I say, surely there's no harm in trying?

Chamberlain No.

Halifax And even if it does prove impossible, at least France will then not be able to say that we stood between her and a tolerable settlement. Or worse, use that as an excuse for making a separate peace.

Churchill Yes, well, I see the force of that.

Pause.

Very well. I raise no objection to some approach being made to Signor Mussolini. But it should be carefully worded.

Halifax smiles with relief.

Halifax Thank you, Prime Minister. I shall draft one for the Cabinet's perusal.

Churchill nods but seems uncomfortable.

Assuming that's all right with our Labour colleagues here of course.

Churchill Yes, of course.

He looks to Attlee and Greenwood. Attlee looks to Greenwood too.

Greenwood Well, I don't like it, and neither will the public if they get to hear of it –

Churchill Well, they mustn't.

Greenwood No.

He looks to Attlee.

Then I suppose we'd better give it a go.

Attlee thinks for a moment before nodding.

Attlee We have no objection, Prime Minister.

Halifax smiles.

What information should be given to the Dominions, though?

Churchill Nothing in regard to the discussions with Monsieur Reynaud. But they should be told that we have now obtained the formal assent of the French Government to fall back on the coast, and that the position is a serious one.

Attlee nods.

Until tomorrow then, gentlemen.

The others nod, get up and go.
Churchill remains with Jock.
He seems unsettled and agitated as he thinks what to do.
Pause as the lights then cross-fade to the front of the stage as Halifax and Chamberlain walk away from Number Ten into St James's Park.

Halifax Well . . . that went better than I expected.

Chamberlain (*surprised*) Really?

Halifax Yes, he was almost reasonable for a change. Or at least, not unreasonable.

Chamberlain smiles weakly.

But he does have the most disorderly mind I think I've ever seen. A child's emotion with a man's intellect.

Chamberlain . . . I know what you mean.

They pause at the front of the stage and look out at the park.

Halifax Still, at least he's prepared to negotiate at last. That's the main thing.

Chamberlain Yes, well, we have no choice now, do we?

Halifax No . . .

Pause.

So we must try and reach a settlement, however distasteful it may be, while we still have allies, and an army, to bargain with . . . Otherwise . . . well, it won't just be a few colonies we could lose, but this whole . . . (*he looks around*) 'green and pleasant land' . . .

Chamberlain Yes . . . if the war goes on as it has been, Hitler could be in London by July.

They take in the horror of this.
Then Halifax flinches.

Halifax Oh, it doesn't bear thinking about, does it?

Chamberlain No . . . But we must, so that others don't have to. That's what government is.

Halifax Yes . . .

Pause.

Well . . . I'd better go and write that draft, hadn't I?

Chamberlain Indeed . . .

They turn to go.

But do show it to me before Cabinet if you like.

Halifax Thank you. I will.

They walk away.

But thank God it seems Winston is finally coming round to our point of view . . .

Chamberlain considers this.

Chamberlain (*sceptically*) Mm . . .

Halifax I just hope it's not too late . . .

And they go off looking concerned as the lights cross-fade back to the Cabinet room, where Churchill is still deep in thought.
Long pause.
Then suddenly he speaks.

Churchill Jock, take down the following question for the Chief of the Imperial General Staff.

Jock gets his pen and pad ready.

Jock Yes, sir.

Churchill thinks.

Churchill In the event of France being unable to continue in the war, and becoming neutral . . . with the Germans holding their present position, and the Belgian army being forced to capitulate after helping the British Expeditionary Force to reach the coast . . . and in the event of terms being offered to Britain which would place her entirely at the mercy of Germany through disarmament, cession of naval bases, etc. . . . . what are our chances of continuing the war alone? . . . And more particularly, of resisting invasion?

Jock finishes writing.

Have you got that?

Jock Yes, Prime Minister.

Churchill Good. Now tell him I want him to present it to the Cabinet tomorrow.

Jock Yes, sir.

> *Churchill picks up his gas mask and goes out.*
> *Jock pauses for a moment as he takes in what's been said, before picking up the pad and following him out.*
> *The lights fade.*

SCENE THREE

Monday, the 27 May. Afternoon.
> *The sound of Big Ben chiming four times.*
> *Then the lights fade up on the War Cabinet in progress. No one is saying anything.*
> *There is a tense atmosphere as people smoke and fiddle with pens, etc.*
> *Then General Dill – fifty-eight, tall and grey – enters, carrying a folder under his arm. Jock follows behind him and closes the door before going to his desk to take minutes.*

Churchill Ah, thank you for joining us, General.

Dill Prime Minister . . . (*He nods at the others.*) Gentlemen . . .

> *The others respond.*

Churchill Now perhaps you could start by telling us the current position regarding our withdrawal to Dunkirk?

Dill Of course.

Dill goes over to the map and indicates the positions as he talks.

Well, the BEF are in good heart, with the remainder of two divisions protecting the approaches to Dunkirk and the Belgian army protecting our left flank, where they've been putting up good resistance and have taken some prisoners.

Pleased responses from the Cabinet.

Withdrawal to Dunkirk, however, will take two or three days, and those days will be extremely critical . . . The gap through which we can withdraw is very narrow, and only two roads are available, both of which remain clogged with refugees . . . However, naval vessels are now standing by to cover re-embarkation in the Dunkirk area.

Nods from the Cabinet.

Meanwhile, our troops in Calais are still holding out with great gallantry. It will be recalled that on Friday last the Brigadier in command had been given one hour to surrender.

Churchill Yes . . .

A concerned pause.

And how many do you think we can get away once they get to Dunkirk?

Dill Well, it must be said we aren't optimistic. Once gathered there, we fear we will make an easy target for the German tanks and aircraft, and re-embarkation will be a slow and difficult process. And, of course, if the jetties are hit, we will be entirely dependent on smaller vessels to take the men directly off the beaches . . .

Churchill How many?

Dill . . . Only a small portion, I'm afraid. Perhaps a few thousand.

Churchill Out of a quarter of a million?

Dill Yes.

They take this in.

Attlee Yes, well, that's what they said in the last war about the Gallipoli evacuation, but quite a few of us got out of there all right.

Churchill Mm . . .

Churchill doesn't seem very cheered.

Well, in any event, we must make sure we give no priority to our troops over the French, but must go arm in arm with them if we are to save the Alliance.

Dill Yes, sir. Of course.

Pause.

Churchill Now, as regards the question I put to you yesterday . . . If the worst comes to the worst and the French go down, taking most of the BEF with them, can we fight on alone or can't we?

Dill opens the folder he's been holding.

Dill Well, I have here the Report of the Chiefs of Staff Committee, 'British Strategy in a Certain Eventuality'.

Churchill can't help a smile.

Churchill What a charming euphemism.

Dill Yes . . . Anyway, I'd like to summarise the main points for you, if I may.

Churchill Certainly.

Dill Thank you.

He consults the report.

While our Air Force is in being, our Navy and Air Force together should be able to prevent Germany carrying out a serious seaborne invasion of this country.

Beat.

Supposing Germany gains complete air superiority, we think the Navy could still hold up an invasion for a time, but not for an indefinite period.

Beat.

If, however, with our Navy unable to prevent it and our Air Force gone, Germany attempted an invasion, our coast and beach defences could not prevent German tanks and infantry getting a firm footing on our shores. And in those circumstances our land forces would be insufficient to deal with a serious invasion. Germany will have at least seventy divisions available for invasion, and we . . . no more than fifteen with which to resist.

Glances around the table.

The crux of the matter then is air superiority.

Nods and 'Mm's of understanding from the Cabinet.

Now Germany cannot gain complete air superiority unless she knocks out both our Air Force and our aircraft industries, some vital portions of which are concentrated at Coventry and Birmingham. Can she do this?

He looks at them.

Well, of course, air attacks on the aircraft factories could be made by day, or by night . . . By *day*, we think that we should be able to inflict such casualties on the enemy as to prevent serious damage. However, whatever we do by way of defensive measures – and we are pressing on with these with all despatch – we cannot be sure of protecting the large industrial centres upon which our aircraft industries depend from serious material damage by *night* attack.

Beat.

Of course, whether the attacks succeed in eliminating the aircraft industry depends not only on the material damage by bombs but on the moral effect on the workpeople and their determination to carry on in the face of wholesale havoc and destruction.

He pauses.

If however the enemy presses home night attacks on our aircraft industry, he is likely to achieve such material and moral damage within the industrial area concerned as to bring all work to a standstill.

Beat.

And it must be remembered that numerically the Germans have a superiority in aircraft of four to one.

Churchill reacts. The others look solemn.

To sum up, our conclusion is that *prima facie* the Germans have most of the cards . . . But the real test is whether the morale of our fighting personnel and civil population will counterbalance the numerical and material advantages Germany enjoys . . . We, of course, believe it will.

He closes his folder.

Churchill Thank you, General.

Beat.

May I make one observation, though? In saying that the Germans have an air superiority of four to one you are comparing our operational strength to their first line strength. According to my figures, on a true basis of comparison the odds against us are only two and a half to one.

Dill (*sceptical*) Really . . . ?

Churchill Yes. Moreover, if, in addition, our airmen are shooting down three to one, as they have been in France, then overall the balance is on our side, is it not?

Dill Possibly. But at night the balance will be very much less favourable for us. It is only in the day fighting that we are able to inflict such heavy losses on the enemy. At night, as we have seen with our bombing of Germany, there are very few losses . . . So there seems little doubt that it might well be possible for the Germans to stop all work in our aircraft factories, and it is only right that I should make this clear to you . . . Even on dark nights the German bombers would be able to find big areas like Coventry and bomb them indiscriminately. And if the Germans escort their bombers by large numbers of fighters, we should be at a disadvantage even in the daytime, owing to our inferior strength, whether it is four to one or two and a half to one.

Churchill thinks.

Churchill What about a counter-offensive against German oil and aircraft factories?

Dill That would have some effect, but unfortunately the German factories are widely dispersed and situated in distant parts of Germany where they are far less vulnerable than our own.

Churchill Hm . . .

He looks concerned.

Well, thank you, General. And unless anyone else has any questions they'd like to ask . . .

Dill hesitates.

Halifax Yes, if I may, Prime Minister . . .?

Churchill Of course.

Halifax Thank you.

He turns to Dill.

General, you say in your conclusion that you believe that our morale might save us.

Dill Yes . . .

Halifax But how, I wonder, is that consistent with the point you make that 'if the enemy press home night attacks on our aircraft industry, he is likely to achieve such material and *moral* damage . . . as to bring all work to a standstill'?

Dill hesitates.

Dill Well . . . in truth, I'm not sure it is. But, well, we must hope for the best, mustn't we?

Halifax smiles.

Halifax Mm . . .

Looks of concern pass round the room.

Churchill Anyone else?

The others shake their heads gravely.

Then you may go now, General. And thank you.

Dill nods and goes.
Churchill thinks.
Pause.

Halifax If I may, Prime Minister, perhaps now is the time to show the Cabinet the draft approach to Italy you asked me to prepare?

Churchill Yes. Go ahead.

Halifax Thank you.

He takes out his memorandum.

So. I suggest that together with the French we make a direct approach to Signor Mussolini on the following lines.

He glances at his memorandum.

Firstly, a frank explanation of the position in which Signor Mussolini will be placed if the Germans establish domination in Europe . . . Secondly, an assurance that Great Britain and France will fight to the end for the preservation of their independence . . . But thirdly, if Signor Mussolini will co-operate with us in securing a settlement of all European questions which *safeguards* the independence and security of the allies and could be the basis of a just and durable peace, then we will undertake at once to discuss, with the desire to find solutions, the matters in which Signor Mussolini is primarily interested . . . adding that we understand that he desires the solution of certain Mediterranean questions. And if he will state in secrecy what these are, France and Great Britain will at once do their best to meet his wishes, on the basis of co-operation set out above.

Chamberlain nods.

Chamberlain Mm . . . that sounds reasonable.

All look to Churchill, who looks unhappy but says nothing as he ruminates.

Halifax Prime Minister?

Churchill Mm?

Halifax Are you happy with my proposed wording?

Churchill Happy? (*He thinks.*) No. Happy is not the right word.

Halifax smiles tolerantly.

Halifax Prime Minister . . . may I send it to Monsieur Reynaud?

Churchill hesitates.
He looks at Chamberlain, who shrugs as if to say, what choice do we have?
Then a knock at the door.
They are surprised.

Churchill See who it is, will you, Jock?

Jock goes to the door, opens it for a moment, then closes it and takes a piece of paper to Churchill.

Jock A telegram from Paris, sir.

Churchill Ah. Speak of the devil . . .

He takes and reads it.

Yes, it's from Monsieur Reynaud. And he says . . . I won't attempt the accent . . .

Smiles from the others.

(*Reading.*) 'I thank you for your cordial welcome yesterday. Your friendship is precious to me . . . As for Italy, the assistance given by your country to mine through the approach we are making at this tragic hour will help to strengthen an alliance of hearts which I believe to be essential.'

Beat.

Mm . . .

Halifax Well, I think that's very nice. We have strengthened our alliance with France. What possible harm could there be in that?

Chamberlain Indeed.

Churchill I don't know . . .

He thinks.

(*With feeling.*) But I don't like it . . . I don't like it at all.

Halifax looks at Chamberlain in exasperation.

Halifax You don't like it?

Churchill No. He writes as if we've agreed to it, which we haven't yet.

Halifax looks concerned.

Halifax No, but we're going to, aren't we?

He looks at Churchill, who looks at the telegram again.

We have no choice.

Churchill looks up at him quickly.

Churchill There's always a choice.

They look at each other for a moment.
Then Churchill looks away.

And as it happens . . . well, I'm becoming increasingly oppressed with the futility of it all.

He casts the telegram aside.
Halifax looks perturbed.

Halifax Futility?

Churchill Yes. Signor Mussolini would be bound to regard it with contempt as he's never forgiven us for opposing his invasion of Abyssinia.

Halifax Well, I really don't think that will –

Churchill And in any case I can't help thinking that such an approach would do Monsieur Reynaud far less good than if he made a firm stand.

Greenwood intervenes.

Greenwood Hear, hear.

Halifax is appalled by this outburst.
But Churchill, encouraged, exchanges a glance with Greenwood, stands up and begins walking round the room.

Churchill Most importantly though, it would ruin the integrity of our fighting position in this country. And even if we did not include geographical precision and mentioned no names, everybody would know what we had in mind.

Greenwood Of course they would.

No one can deny this.

Churchill So let us not be dragged down with the French. If they are not prepared to go on with the struggle, let them give up, though I doubt whether they will. If *this* country is beaten though, France becomes a vassal state . . . But if we win, we might save them. So the best help we can give to Monsieur Reynaud is to let him feel that, whatever happens to France, we are going to fight it out to the end.

Greenwood Absolutely.

Halifax Well –

Churchill Let me finish, please.

Halifax reluctantly makes way.

Thank you. You see, at the moment our prestige in Europe is very low. And the only way we can get it back is by showing the world that Germany has not beaten us . . . If, after two or three months, we can show that we are still unbeaten, our prestige will return . . . And even if we are beaten, we should be no worse off than if we were to abandon the struggle now . . . Indeed, if the worst comes to the worst, it will be no bad thing for this country to go down fighting for the other countries that have been overcome by the Nazi tyranny.

Halifax can't believe what he's hearing.

So let us avoid being dragged down the slippery slope with France. This whole manoeuvre is intended to get us so deeply involved in negotiations that we will be unable to turn back . . . So the approach is not only futile, but involves us in a deadly danger that could lead to disaster.

Greenwood I agree. It reminds me of September last year. There was talk of an Italian option then too. But what we must do is as clear now as it was then. Fight.

He looks to Attlee who begins to nod with understanding.
 Halifax is horrified.
 He looks to Chamberlain for support.
 Then gathers himself.

Halifax . . . I am conscious of certain rather profound differences of points of view between the Prime Minister and myself which I would like to make clear.

Beat.

In the first place, I would have thought that, if we could persuade them to do so, there would be some positive value in getting the French Government to say that they will fight to the end for their independence.

Chamberlain nods.

Chamberlain True . . .

Halifax Secondly, I cannot recognise any resemblance between the action I propose and the suggestion that we are following a line which could lead to disaster. On the contrary, the risk of disaster lies in not taking the action I propose.

Beat.

The Prime Minister has said that two or three months would show whether we were able to stand up against the air risk. But this would mean that the future of the country turned on whether the enemy's bombs happened to hit our aircraft factories. I am prepared to take that risk if our independence is at stake. But if it is not, I would think it right to accept an offer which would save the country from avoidable disaster.

Chamberlain nods.

Lastly . . . in the discussion yesterday I asked the Prime Minister whether, if he was satisfied that matters vital to the independence of this country were unaffected, he would be prepared to discuss terms, and the Prime Minister said that he would be 'thankful' to get out of our present difficulties even at the cost of some territory.

Churchill cannot deny it.

Today, however, he seems to suggest that under no conditions would he contemplate any course except fighting to a finish . . . If, however, it is possible to obtain a settlement which did not impair those conditions, I, for my part, doubt if I would be able to accept the view now put forward by the Prime Minister . . .

A frisson passes through the Cabinet.
Halifax looks to Chamberlain, who looks deeply concerned by this turn of events.
Churchill too is alarmed.
Impasse.
All look to Chamberlain.

Churchill Mr Chamberlain?

Chamberlain Yes, well . . . whilst of course I agree that that there is no guarantee that the proposed approach will succeed, I, like the Foreign Secretary, think we ought to at least give it a try.

*Greenwood shakes his head and Churchill looks
disappointed.
Chamberlain sees this.
Another impasse.*

But perhaps we all need a night to sleep on it?

*Halifax is put out by this suggestion.
Chamberlain looks apologetic.*

Attlee Yes, I think we do.

Greenwood All right then.

Churchill Foreign Secretary?

Halifax If you wish. But we can't put it off for ever. The
French are expecting a reply and the sooner we give
them one the better.

Churchill Yes, well . . . we shall make a final decision
tomorrow then. Without fail. Good evening, gentlemen.

*They get up to go.
Churchill hesitates.*

Edward, could I have a word?

Halifax . . . Of course.

Churchill Thank you.

The others leave.

But it's got rather hot in here. Let's go out into the garden.

Halifax Very well.

*They walk out of the room to the front of the stage
and the lights change to a warm evening light.*

Churchill What a beautiful evening.

Halifax Yes . . . Somewhat ironic, isn't it?

Churchill Mm . . .

Pause.

Look, Edward, this country is in the tightest corner it's ever been in, isn't it?

Halifax Yes, I think it is. Since 1066 at any rate.

Churchill Well then, we must, at all costs, stick together, mustn't we?

Halifax hesitates.

Halifax Of course.

Beat.

But if we were to give up a chance, perhaps a slim one I admit, but a chance of peace on reasonable terms . . . well, how can I support that?

Churchill hesitates but realises that he's not going to change his mind.

Churchill Look, Edward, we may disagree. But you mustn't resign.

He looks at him.

Two weeks ago, when all this started, you had the chance to be Prime Minister. Neville wanted you to succeed him. The King wanted you. The Party wanted you. But you decided you didn't want it.

Halifax You can't be Prime Minister and in the House of Lords.

Churchill Yes, yes. So you say.

Halifax And the country wanted you . . .

Churchill Well, perhaps. But in any case, you let me become PM. And then you graciously agreed to continue serving as Foreign Secretary. But now two weeks later, when the going has got rough, rougher than it's ever been, you threaten to abandon me. What effect would that have on the country at this dark hour – the darkest in our history – if the men at the top can't stick together? So, we must stick together, whatever our differences . . . If you abandon me now, abandon the Cabinet now, who would that benefit but our enemies?

Pause.
  Halifax thinks.

Halifax Very well. I won't resign.

Churchill is relieved.

Churchill Good.

Beat.

Halifax But if you'd just try and be less . . . emotional about it all. Less theatrical. And just think it through clearly. Dispassionately.

Churchill Dispassionately?

Halifax Yes.

Churchill smiles.

Churchill Can a leopard change its spots?

Halifax can't help smiling.

Halifax No, I suppose not. You are nothing if not passionate, Winston.

They smile.

But you must be reasonable too.

Churchill I know. I get carried away. And put things too strongly sometimes. But you must forgive my rhetorical flourishes. It comes from writing too many books . . . But that's why I need you so much. I need you and Neville to keep my feet on the ground. You are the wise old elephants who must look after and restrain the rogue elephant.

36

Halifax Yes, well, sometimes the weight seems more than we can bear.

Churchill smiles.
  A thought occurs to Halifax.

May I ask you one question though?

Churchill Of course.

Halifax thinks how to phrase it.

Halifax Can you conceive of any circumstances in which you think it would be right *not* to go on fighting? If not to surrender, or even negotiate, at least, say, for the King and Government to go to Canada and continue the fight from there?

Churchill thinks.

Churchill In truth, no, I don't think I can. In my view, every man ought really to fight to the death on his own soil . . . So if the Germans come to London, I shall take a rifle – I'm not a bad shot with a rifle – and put myself in the pillbox at the bottom of Downing Street and shoot till I've no more ammunition, and then they can damned well shoot me.

Halifax takes this in.

Halifax And what about our women and children?

Churchill Well, if we run out of guns, they can use kitchen knives and suchlike. But everyone who can ought to at least try and take a German down with them.

Halifax I see. Well, I hope you understand if we don't all feel that way. And at least want our wives and children to survive. Not to mention our whole way of life . . .

Churchill Of course.

Halifax Well, that is what I'm trying to preserve.

He thinks.

So I ask just one thing of you.

Churchill What?

He chooses his words carefully.

Halifax If Neville also wishes to approach Italy, you allow us to do so?

Churchill looks concerned.

You at least owe us that, don't you?

Churchill hesitates.

Churchill And if I refuse?

Halifax shrugs.

Halifax I resign.

Churchill takes this in.

Of course, I can't speak for Neville . . .

Pause.
Churchill hesitates before making a decision.

Churchill Very well.

Halifax smiles with relief.

Halifax Thank you.

Pause.

Now, I must go. I'm meeting my wife for dinner at the Dorchester.

Churchill Ah, then you mustn't keep her waiting.

Halifax No.

Beat.

See you tomorrow then.

Churchill Yes, good night.

Halifax Good night.

Halifax goes, feeling confident that his view will now prevail.
Pause.
Churchill hesitates for a moment.
Then walks back into the Cabinet room.

Churchill Get me a whisky and soda, please, Jock. Very weak.

Jock Of course, sir.

Jock makes him a Johnnie Walker whisky and soda as Churchill thinks.
Then Jock hands him the drink.

Churchill Thank you.

He takes a long drink.

Now send the following message to Lord Gort.

Jock gets his pen and paper ready.
Churchill thinks.

At this solemn moment I cannot help sending you my best wishes . . . No one can tell how it will go. But anything is better than being cooped up and starved out . . . Presume troops know they are cutting their way home to Blighty. Never was there such a spur for fighting . . . We shall give you all that the Navy and Air Force can do.

Jock finishes writing and looks up at him.

(*To Jock.*) And tell Brigadier Nicholson at Calais that the eyes of the Empire are on him. And that he must fight on to the bitter end.

He reflects bitterly as Jock writes this down.

That's all. Now I must have dinner. After all, one must eat and drink even in war.

He drains his drink and is about to go when something occurs to him.

Oh, one more thing.

He hesitates.

Ask Mr Chamberlain to come and see me half an hour before Cabinet tomorrow.

Jock Yes, sir.

Churchill Thank you.

He picks up the red box.

Good night, Jock.

Jock Good night, sir.

Churchill goes.
Jock is left alone on the stage as he reflects.
Then he takes a card and begins writing a note to Chamberlain as the lights fade.

Act Two

SCENE ONE

Tuesday, the 28 May.
  Morning.
  The sound of Big Ben chiming nine times.
  Then the lights come up downstage as Jock walks on,
holding a notebook, and faces the audience.

Jock This is what I wrote in my diary.

He opens it and reads.

Tuesday, 28th May . . . I still feel convinced that we will
win, even if the French collapse. But we have reached all
but the last ditch and a timely miracle would be
acceptable.

He pauses for a moment and smiles.
  Then continues.

For my own part, I have decided that if the war continues,
I must make a determined effort to go and fight, though
I know the PM won't want to lose me. However, in
present circumstances what is reasonable must take
second place to what one's conscience dictates. I will
move heaven and earth to go.

He closes the book and smiles at his younger self.
  Then steps into the Cabinet room and goes over to
his desk.
  He sits down, opens a drawer, puts the diary inside
and closes the drawer again.
  Then takes a key out of his pocket, locks the
drawer and puts the key back in his pocket.
  He then opens the Prime Minister's red box and
begins sorting through the papers when the door

opens and Chamberlain enters, carrying his hat and umbrella.

Chamberlain Ah, good morning, Jock.

Jock Good morning, Pri—

He checks himself.

Mr Chamberlain.

Chamberlain smiles.

Chamberlain You didn't know what to call me, did you?

Jock Well, I must admit, it seems odd calling you Mr Chamberlain. After calling you Prime Minister for so long.

Chamberlain Yes, well, it seems odd to me too. But it's now eighteen days since I was Prime Minister. Eighteen of the longest days of my life.

He reflects.

Anyway, I take it the Prime Minister hasn't arrived yet?

Jock No, I believe he's still at the Admiralty.

Chamberlain Ah. Yes, well, I must say, it was kind of him to let me and Mrs Chamberlain stay on here till things quieten down a bit. If they ever do. But it does feel, as you say, odd, still living here but no longer being, as it were, master of the house. Let alone the country.

He smiles at Jock, who smiles back.

Bad news about the Belgians, isn't it?

Jock Yes, sir.

Chamberlain Though it was hardly unexpected. Still, it would have been nice if they could have held out just a little longer. After all, we did go over there to try and save them.

Jock Yes . . .

Pause.

Chamberlain But do carry on with your work. I'll just wait here till he arrives.

Jock Thank you, sir.

Jock goes back to his work as Chamberlain waits for a moment in the middle of the room, tapping his umbrella.
Then looks at his watch.
Finally, he puts his hat and umbrella down and goes over to the bookcase.
There he spots a book, hesitates for a moment, then takes it out.
He looks at it and feels it in such a way that makes it clear it has some special significance for him.
Then he opens it and begins to read.
He stops for a moment and smiles at the memory of something.
Then he reads on before stopping again, but this time with sadness and concern. Whatever he's read has shaken him to the core and he can no longer even look at the book.
At this point the door opens and Churchill enters briskly.

Churchill Ah, Neville, you're already here. Good. You got my message then?

Chamberlain Yes.

Churchill Thank you for coming.

Chamberlain Not at all.

Churchill sees the book in his hands.

Churchill Been reading have you? Good idea. Take your mind off things for a while. What was it? Something from our glorious past?

43

Chamberlain Well . . . not exactly.

Churchill How do you mean?

Chamberlain Actually, it's my own book. *The Struggle for Peace.*

Churchill Ah . . . yes.

Chamberlain It now sounds rather, well . . . (*He thinks.*) I suppose hubristic is the word, isn't it?

Churchill smiles uncomfortably.

Churchill Well, perhaps a trifle optimistic.

Chamberlain Yes, that too. Or naive, you might say. Probably did say . . . What was your book called again?

Churchill *While England Slept.*

Chamberlain Yes. A much better title, I now think . . . and book too.

Churchill Well . . .

Chamberlain Anyway, listen to this.

He lifts up the book and reads.

'If things go wrong the Prime Minister can never escape the reflection "I might have prevented this if I had thought or acted differently".'

He reflects.

Churchill Yes, well . . . we must all take our share of responsibility.

Chamberlain Yes, I suppose. Or at least, all except you.

He looks at Churchill.

You understood Hitler from the start, didn't you? And warned me he was a madman. So you must blame me for not understanding him? I should have listened to you, shouldn't I?

Churchill hesitates.

Churchill I blame your predecessors more. Baldwin and MacDonald did nothing for five years but preach disarmament to the French whilst practising it on the British. They are the ones who lost air parity and allowed Hitler to reoccupy the Rhineland when a mere show of force would have been sufficient to repel him. Supported by the Labour and Liberal parties, I might add.

Chamberlain Yes.

Churchill At least you made a start.

Chamberlain More than a start . . . And crucially, what I won for us was, if not 'peace in our time', at least *more* time. A whole year more, which at least gives us a chance. We wouldn't have had a hope in . . . well, a hope, a year ago.

Churchill Well, I'm afraid I can't agree with you there.

Chamberlain Why? Our defences and Air Force were nothing to what they are now?

Churchill True. But if we'd gone to war when the Germans threatened Czechoslovakia they'd have had only thirteen divisions available to protect the whole of their western Front against a a hundred French divisions, since they'd have needed most of their army to deal with a million and half Czechs entrenched behind the strongest fortress line in Europe. Instead, though, we forced the Czechs to back down and allowed Hitler to continue picking off his targets one by one.

Chamberlain *(taken aback)* Yes, well, I still think it was worthwhile making our Air Force ten times stronger than it was then . . . or at any rate, it's at least arguable.

Churchill *(sceptically)* Mm . . .

But he resists continuing the argument.

But look, there's no point going back over that now, is there? This isn't the time for a post mortem. Not while we're fighting for our life.

Chamberlain No . . .

Churchill So we must look to the future. And deal with the present. Which is what I wanted to talk to you about.

Chamberlain Of course.

Chamberlain puts his book back on the shelf.

Churchill Now, forgive me for speaking bluntly, but it seems clear, does it not, from the last two days of discussion that Edward wants to do a deal with Hitler, casting Mussolini in the role of mediator as he was at Munich.

Chamberlain Well, I wouldn't put it in quite those words, but I suppose, yes, that is the essence of his position. Though he would not, of course, accept unreasonable terms. And neither would I, of course.

He looks at Churchill, making it clear whose side he's on.

Churchill Very well. Suppose, for the sake of argument, that Hitler was prepared to offer us terms we could accept . . . How could we trust him to stick to those terms? Surely, if we've learned anything from Munich, it's that Hitler cannot be trusted to keep his word.

Chamberlain True. His word is worth nothing. As I know better than anyone . . . But if he does not wish to fight us, as he may not, then he will keep it nonetheless.

Churchill And allow us to remain in command of the sea and the vast part of our Empire? I do not think that likely, do you?

Chamberlain thinks.

Chamberlain Perhaps not, but –

Churchill On the other hand, suppose that he breaks his word and we find again that it is time to fight. Then surely our resolve will be weaker than it is now and his strength, having consolidated his position in France, greater?

Chamberlain thinks.

Chamberlain That is possible.

Churchill Indeed. Which is why I asked you to come and see me this morning.

He looks him in the eye.

Neville, I need your support in this matter, to avoid such an outcome.

Chamberlain is surprised.

Chamberlain You're asking me to side with you against Edward?

Churchill On this matter, yes.

Chamberlain takes this in.

There has never been a decision more vital to our country.

Chamberlain I know that.

Churchill Of course.

Chamberlain thinks.

Chamberlain And if I don't?

Churchill Well, even if our Labour colleagues supported me, I wouldn't feel I could carry through a decision of this magnitude without you.

Chamberlain looks concerned.

Chamberlain So what would you do?

Churchill hesitates.

Churchill Well, since you force me to consider the possibility . . . I think I would have no alternative but to resign.

Chamberlain is appalled.

Chamberlain Resign?

Churchill Yes. What else could I do?

Chamberlain takes this in.

There can be no bigger decision for a Prime Minister, as you know, than whether or not to wage war. So it follows that if he cannot command the support of his Cabinet, either he or they must go. And I do not propose that you and Edward should be sacrificed, carrying as you do the full support of the dominant party in Parliament.

Chamberlain thinks.

Chamberlain You mustn't resign.

Churchill But how could I not in those circumstances?

Chamberlain But you have the full support of the country at large.

Churchill Perhaps. But it was you who got the bigger cheer when we entered the House that first time after we swapped places . . . So what choice would I have if I no longer had your support in this most vital matter?

Beat.

Or are you asking me to go against my conscience and all I have stood for by leading us into what amounts to a second Munich?

Chamberlain reacts.

Anyway, it's up to you, Neville. I am in your hands. The country is in your hands. And far be it from me to tell you what you must do. But I thought it was as well to let you know of the consequences before Cabinet.

Chamberlain Yes . . . thank you.

He looks troubled.
There is a knock at the door.

Churchill Come in.

Attlee and Greenwood enter, but hesitate when they see Chamberlain.

Ah, our Labour colleagues.

Attlee Yes, um, actually, we were hoping to have a quick word with you, Prime Minister. Before the Cabinet.

Churchill Well, I have no secrets from Mr Chamberlain.

Attlee (*uncomfortable*) Yes, well . . . actually, we'd prefer to speak to you alone. If possible.

Greenwood Yes.

They all look at Chamberlain.

Chamberlain Then I shall take a walk round the park . . . I could do with some air in any case . . .

Churchill Thank you.

Chamberlain picks up his hat and umbrella.

Chamberlain See you shortly.

He goes off thoughtfully.
Pause.

Churchill Well, gentlemen. What can I do for you?

Attlee and Greenwood look at each other.

Attlee Prime Minister, we're very concerned about this Italian proposal.

Churchill Indeed?

Greenwood Yes. We can't understand why we need to have yet another Cabinet meeting about it.

Churchill You can't?

Attlee No. It's clear what a disastrous effect it would have on the country.

Greenwood Absolutely. The unions won't stand for it.

Attlee The people want to fight. And yet Halifax and Chamberlain continue to support this craven approach to Italy and you refuse to kick it into touch once and for all where it belongs.

Greenwood And we have a clear majority of three against two.

Attlee Exactly. We agreed to serve under you, not them, and we wouldn't have if we'd known those two appeasers were still going to dictate policy.

Greenwood The architects of this catastrophe.

Attlee The 'guilty men' of Munich.

They pause, satisfied that they have made their point.

Churchill Yes, well, I seem to recall there were a lot of appeasers in the House that night Mr Chamberlain returned from Munich.

Churchill glances at them pointedly and Attlee and Greenwood look suitably embarrassed.

So we must pass a sponge across the past. Because, as I have said before, if the present tries to sit in judgement on the past, we shall lose the future.

He looks at them meaningfully.

But I thank you for speaking so plainly to me, gentlemen. It's heartening to know I have your support in this matter. But do you not see how important it is that we retain our colleagues' support too? Mr Chamberlain is still leader of the Conservative Party, who, whatever popularity the Labour Party may have achieved in the country, still dominate the Commons. So if we cannot carry Chamberlain with us, we cannot carry Parliament. And if we cannot carry Parliament, well, we are doomed.

Greenwood But so we are if we go against the wishes of the country. And the country wants to fight.

Churchill Quite. So we must bring Mr Chamberlain round to our point of view. Which is what I was trying to do before you arrived . . . But we cannot afford to alienate him. He is still a very powerful man. And we must be patient with him.

Attlee But time is of the essence in this matter. As even Halifax recognises. A decision must be made and we can't afford to wait any longer.

Greenwood No.

Churchill You are right. And we shall have to make one before the day is out . . . one way or the other.

They look at him with concern.
The door opens suddenly and Halifax enters.
Attlee and Greenwood glance at him uncomfortably.

Halifax Oh, sorry, am I late?

He checks his watch.

Churchill No, not at all. Perfectly on time. As always.

Halifax Good.

An awkward pause.

Ah yes, and I see Neville hasn't arrived yet.

Churchill No . . . uh, he's just taking a turn around the park.

Halifax Ah . . . to clear his head perhaps?

Churchill Yes.

Halifax Well, we all need to do that sometimes.

Churchill Indeed.

An awkward pause.
   Then Chamberlain enters.

Ah, good. Here he is.

Halifax smiles at Chamberlain.

Halifax Good morning, Neville.

Chamberlain Edward . . .

Churchill is pained by their easy intimacy and exchanges a worried look with Attlee and Greenwood.

Churchill Come then, gentlemen. Let us sit down and begin.

They take their usual seats round the Cabinet table.

Now, as I think you all know, we are here to discuss – for the third and I hope final time – the Foreign Secretary's suggested approach to Italy.

Mumbles of assent.

Halifax Yes. Thank you, Prime Minister.

He glances at Chamberlain.

Now, I wish to start by saying that I agree that there is no guarantee that anything would result from an approach on the lines suggested by the French as Signor Mussolini may refuse to play ball.

Beat.

However, assuming that he does wish to play the part of mediator, and that he can produce terms which would not affect our independence, I for one think that we would be foolish not to consider them, since we simply cannot afford to ignore the fact that we might get better terms before France goes out of the war – as Belgium has now done – and our aircraft factories are bombed, than we might get in three months' time.

He looks at them all intently.

And that, in a nutshell, is the essence of my argument.

He looks to Chamberlain for support.

Churchill Thank you, Foreign Secretary.

He pauses.

To me, however, the essential point is that Monsieur Reynaud wants to get us to the conference table with Herr Hitler. However, once we get to the table, we shall then find that the terms offered us touch our independence and integrity. When, at this point, we get up to leave the conference table, we shall find that all the forces of resolution that are now at our disposal have vanished.

Greenwood Hear, hear.

Churchill thinks.

Churchill The point is the French want to get out of the war, but do not want to break their agreement with us not to make a separate peace.

Greenwood nods.

But if Signor Mussolini comes in as mediator, he will take his whack out of us. And it is impossible to imagine that Herr Hitler would be so foolish as to let us continue our rearmament. In effect, his terms are bound to put us completely at his mercy . . . If, on the other hand, we continue the war and Germany attacks us, no doubt we shall suffer some damage, but they will also suffer severe losses . . . And we shall get no worse terms if we go on fighting, even if we are beaten, than are open to us now.

Greenwood No. It seems to me that any course we take is attended by great danger and the line of resistance is certainly a gamble, but I don't feel this is a time for ultimate capitulation.

Halifax reacts.

Halifax Nothing in my suggestion can even remotely be described as ultimate capitulation.

Greenwood shrugs.

Churchill (*mollifying*) Of course not. But the chances of decent terms being offered to us at the present time are a thousand to one.

Halifax shakes his head.

Halifax I disagree. Now he has got what he wants Hitler should be desperate to make peace with us.

Churchill Yes, well, I dare say he might be, on his own outrageous terms.

Halifax But how can we know they're outrageous if we never hear them?

Churchill frowns.

You see, after all these discussions we've had, I still don't see what it is about the idea of even trying mediation that you feel is so wrong?

He looks at Churchill, who looks back at him.

Churchill Then you never will.

Halifax is surprised.

Halifax No, I don't believe I will.

Pause.
Halifax looks to Chamberlain, who looks troubled. Attlee and Greenwood glance at each other.

Attlee . . . As leader of the Labour Party, I think it is necessary to pay regard to public opinion in this country. The War Cabinet, with full information, have watched the situation in France and Belgium gradually unfold itself. But when the public realise the true position, they will sustain a severe shock. They will have to make a great effort to maintain their morale – (*he glances at Halifax*) as we have – and there is a grave danger that, if we do what France wants, we shall find it impossible to rally the morale of the people.

Greenwood Absolutely. And so far as the industrial centres of the country are concerned – and they're the most important – they will regard anything like weakening on the part of the Government as a disaster.

Halifax But the whole point is that we may thereby avoid a much greater disaster.

Halifax looks to Chamberlain for support.

And we must be realistic about that. I mean, we're about to lose most of our army, for God's sake.

The others react with surprise.

I'm sorry, but it's true.

Churchill Not yet it isn't. And I still hope that we may not . . .

They reflect for a moment.

However, to return to the question at hand, I think we have all made our positions clear now . . . except you, Mr Chamberlain?

All eyes turn to Chamberlain, but he still seems reluctant to speak.

(*Inviting him to speak.*) Please . . .

Chamberlain looks at him but still seems reluctant to speak.

He seems to be almost in pain as he finally does so.

Chamberlain Yes, well . . . as the Foreign Secretary says . . . it is our duty to look at the situation realistically . . . And I must say, I agree with him that if it is possible we might get terms which, although grievous, would not threaten our independence, we should consider them.

He pauses.
Halifax looks pleased, the others disappointed.

However, looking at the matter realistically, I do not think that it can be said that an approach to Signor Mussolini on the lines proposed by the French would be likely to produce such an offer, certainly not with Paris in Herr Hitler's grasp, but uncaptured. And I therefore conclude that it is not worth making such an approach at the present time.

Halifax is appalled, the others delighted.
Chamberlain finds it hard to look at him.

Greenwood Hear, hear.

Churchill is relieved.

Churchill (*with feeling to Chamberlain*) Thank you.

Chamberlain acknowledges this.
Halifax sees this and smarts.

Chamberlain But I think we must be very careful as to the wording of our answer or France may give up the struggle immediately.

Churchill Of course.

Beat.

Well, I think that concludes our discussion. We shall reject Monsieur Reynaud's proposal.

He gets up.

Now, I must now go down to the House and address the full Cabinet. So if you would care to follow me, gentlemen . . . ?

Attlee Of course.

Greenwood With pleasure, Prime Minister.

Churchill goes out followed by Jock, Attlee and Greenwood.
Chamberlain is about to go too when Halifax speaks.

Halifax Neville, could I have a word, please?

Chamberlain Of course.

Halifax Thank you.

He thinks, somewhat agitated.
Then collects himself.

You know, it's now almost nine months since I watched you sit in that chair and announce to the nation that we were at war with Germany . . . And I remember you saying, 'I cannot believe that there is anything more, or anything different, that I could have done.'

Chamberlain thinks back.

Well, I have rarely been so moved . . . But it is now my turn to make sure that I have done everything I can.

He pauses.

You see, we have now had nine months of war, and all our allies have been defeated, or are about to be – let's face it, *we* have been defeated, where twenty years ago we were victorious in Flanders – and we must ask ourselves once again, is there anything more we can do to prevent the horrors of war?

Beat.

So . . .

He looks at Chamberlain.

We're not really going to let him do this, are we?

Beat.

Chamberlain Do what?

Halifax Throw away our last chance . . . And instead . . . destroy everything. The whole country. The whole Empire.

Chamberlain I believe his aim is the opposite. To save us.

Halifax Perhaps. But so it was in Norway, for which, somehow, you took all the blame and he ended up Prime Minister.

Chamberlain Yes, well, I seem to recall you had something to do with that too.

Halifax I know and I'm beginning to regret it.

He reflects for a moment.

But I thought I could restrain him. I wouldn't have refused the premiership otherwise. But I can't do it on my own.

He looks at him.

I simply don't understand it. Why have you abandoned me? I thought you agreed with me.

Chamberlain hesitates.

Chamberlain It isn't only me. Attlee and Greenwood also think –

Halifax Oh, what do they matter? He'd never dare do this without your support.

He is confused.

And I don't understand why you're giving it to him . . . He's a bully I know, but we must stand up to him.

Beat.

After all, we're all agreed we can't *win* this war and inflict any kind of victory over the Germans. Not unless America comes in. And there seems no hope of that at the moment, whatever Winston may say. So there will be a negotiated peace. It's just a question of when and on what terms. And I reaffirm that we will surely get better terms now than when our Air Force has been defeated, or worse, when we, like France, have been overrun. Not that you and I will be alive then in any case.

Beat.

Chamberlain Perhaps our Air Force won't be defeated?

Halifax Oh, come on, you heard what the Chief of Staff said. Their aircraft outnumber ours by four to one.

Chamberlain But the Prime Minister said –

Halifax The Prime Minister will say anything to continue the war, whatever the cost. For six years before the war he told us the official figures for German aircraft were an underestimate to persuade us to rearm. Now he tells us they are an overestimate to persuade us to fight.

Chamberlain sees the truth of this.

Look, no one can say he lacks nerve, and he certainly knows how to fight. But the trouble is, that's all he knows.

He smiles as a thought strikes him.

You know, I thought for a moment on Sunday, when he spoke of giving up some territory, that he was going to be reasonable for a change. Moderate. But he has clearly reverted to his usual diehard self. Do you know what he told me yesterday evening? That he'd never think it right not to fight and he'd rather be shot in that pillbox at the end of the street than surrender. And he expects the same of everyone else too. Including women and children!

Halifax shakes his head in disbelief.

Death or glory. He knows no other course. Well, in this case, it looks like death. And not only his. But millions of others too . . .

He looks at Chamberlain.

So we must stop him. And we still can. But we must act now or it'll be too late.

He keeps looking at Chamberlain.
Chamberlain thinks.
Pause.

Chamberlain Have I ever told you about my time on a desert island?

Halifax is surprised.

Halifax What?

Chamberlain About the six years I spent in my youth on an almost uninhabited Caribbean island?

Halifax Well, I think I recall something of it, but no, I don't think you've ever . . .

Chamberlain Oh well, I must then.

He thinks back as Halifax looks taken aback.

You see, some time in my early twenties, my father became convinced that our family could make a fortune by growing sisal in the West Indies . . . So in about 1890 my father and brother summoned me from Birmingham to Canada to help them look into it. And after careful reconnaissance from Austen and me, he bought a plot on the island of Andros, but since Austen was the clever one and already due to go into politics, it was left to me to actually set about growing the sisal.

He smiles at the memory as Halifax looks nonplussed.

Well, for six long years I laboured in that lonely spot, swept by hurricanes, living nearly naked, struggling to get and organise the natives and with the town of Nassau the only gleam of civilisation forty miles away across the sea . . . I built a small harbour and landing-stage, and even a short railroad or tramway . . . I used all the processes of fertilisation I judged suitable to the soil, and generally led a completely primitive, open-air existence.

He looks at Halifax.

But after six years, no sisal. Or at least, no sisal fit for the market. So I had to come home and tell my father it was all a failure and a waste of £50,000.

Halifax looks bemused.

But do you know what that taught me?

Halifax thinks.

Halifax Sometimes you have to cut your losses?

Chamberlain Yes. But not until you've given it everything you've got.

Halifax looks concerned.

Halifax We can't give it six years.

Chamberlain hesitates for a moment.

Chamberlain Why not?

Halifax looks at him in a new light.

There are no more deals, Edward. No more Munichs.

Halifax reacts.

I tried that and it didn't work.

Halifax It might this time.

Chamberlain No . . . You weren't there. I was. And he looked into my eyes and promised me he didn't want anything more. And I believed him. But he broke his promise and made a fool of me. So what value is a deal with Hitler anyway?

Halifax To win more time.

Chamberlain What's the point if he's disarmed us?

Halifax Then we won't make a deal.

Chamberlain No. But Winston's right. We shall have to fight some time. And we're better off fighting now. Before we've shown everyone how scared we are.

Their eyes meet.
Pause.

Now come, Edward. We must go. It's time we joined the others and supported the Prime Minister.

He picks up his hat and umbrella and looks at Halifax for a moment.
But Halifax shows no sign of moving.
Chamberlain shrugs and goes out.
Halifax is left alone, isolated and unhappy, before finally, reluctantly, he follows him out.
The lights fade.

SCENE TWO

A committee room in the House of Commons.
A spot comes up on Churchill at the front of the stage as he faces the audience and speaks to the wider Cabinet.
Chamberlain and Halifax join Attlee and Greenwood at the side of the stage as Churchill begins to speak.

Churchill Now, as you all know, the situation in France is very grave. The Belgians have surrendered and France seems on the point of collapse.

Beat.

Hitler will, I expect, take Paris and offer terms, followed by the Italians who will threaten and offer terms. But I have no doubt whatever that we must decline anything like this and fight on . . .

Beat.

We must, though, prepare public opinion for hard and heavy tidings, and it will of course be said – and with some truth – that what is now happening in Northern France is the greatest British military defeat for many centuries.

Beat.

But we must fight our way through to the Channel and get away all we can.

Beat.

How many will get away we cannot tell. I hope we will be able to get fifty thousand away. If we could get a hundred thousand away, that would be a wonderful performance . . . But only Dunkirk is left to us . . . I've just heard that Calais has been lost. It was defended for four days by a British force which refused to surrender, and it is said there are no survivors.

Beat.

Then we must expect the sudden turning of the war against this island, so we must not be taken by surprise. Attempts to invade us will no doubt be made, but they will be beset with immense difficulty. We will mine all round our coast. Our Navy is extremely strong. Our air defences are much more easily organised from this island than across the Channel. Our supplies of food and oil are ample. We have good troops in this island, and others are on the way by sea, both British Army units coming from remote garrisons and excellent Dominion troops. And, as to aircraft, well, it is true that the enemy outnumber us, but we are making good our losses, and they are not. And besides, it is not only quantity that matters. But quality too. And the current battle has proved that, aircraft for aircraft, our fighters are the better.

He thinks.

Now I have thought carefully in these last days whether it was part of my duty to consider entering negotiations with That Man.

Beat.

But it is idle to think that, if we try to make peace now, we will get better terms from Germany than if we go on and fight it out.

He glances at Halifax.

They would demand our fleet – that would be called 'disarmament' – our naval bases, and much else. We would become a slave state, though a British government which would be Hitler's puppet would be set up under Mosley or some such person . . . And where should we be at the end of all that?

He looks around the audience.

Nations which go down fighting rise again, but those which surrender tamely are finished.

Beat.

So whatever happens at Dunkirk, we shall go on and fight it out . . . here . . . or elsewhere if necessary . . . And if at the last our long island story is to end, it is better it should end, not through surrender, but only when we are rolling senseless on the ground. For it is better to perish than to live as slaves.

Shouts of 'Hear, hear' and wild applause.

Chamberlain joins in the applause, but Halifax does not.

Churchill smiles, visibly moved, with tears in his eyes.

The lights fade.

SCENE THREE

Evening.

The lights come up on the Cabinet room in lamplight. It is empty.

Pause.

The door opens and Churchill enters.

He goes over and pours himself a stiff whisky. Then adds water and takes a long drink.

Pause.

He goes over to his cigar box, opens it and takes out a cigar.

He cuts the end off it, puts it in his mouth, lights it and puffs on it.

Then sits down as he drinks and puffs.

Shortly, Jock enters.

Churchill Well, have you sent it?

Jock Yes.

Churchill . . . Good.

Beat.

No going back, then.

He smiles at Jock.

Jock No, sir.

Pause.
  Jock hesitates.

But is it true we might have to evacuate to the country, once the bombing starts?

Churchill No. We're staying right here.

The smoke rises as he takes a puff on his cigar.

And when America sees us standing alone up to Hitler, despite all the bombing and the killing in our cities, then at last she will come to our aid and victory will be ours.

Pause.

You know, Jock, nine months ago, just before war was declared, I called up my old Scotland Yard detective and asked him to come over to Chartwell and bring his pistol with him, since it would have been in accord with the Nazis' usual procedures in other countries if the outbreak of war should be preceded by a sharp prelude of sabotage and murder. And I flattered myself that I might be one of the targets.

He smiles.

Anyway, I got out my weapons too. And while one of us slept the other watched, ensuring that if anybody did try anything, they wouldn't have a walkover . . .

He opens a drawer and takes out a revolver.
  Jock is surprised.
  Churchill sees this and smiles.

Well, that's how I feel tonight too. When Hitler attacks us, he won't have a walkover either.

Jock smiles uncertainly.

Jock No, sir.

Pause.
  Churchill examines his revolver lovingly.
  Jock hesitates.

Look, this may not be a good time, but, uh . . .

Churchill Yes?

Jock Well, there's something I've been wanting to talk to you about.

Churchill Oh yes?

Jock Yes.

Churchill Fine. Now's as good a time as any. Sit down and have a drink.

Jock is surprised. He's never been invited to do this in the Cabinet room before.

Jock Oh . . . Thank you, Prime Minister.

Churchill Help yourself.

Jock Thank you.

He goes over and pours himself a modest whisky and water.
Then brings it to the table and hesitates.

Churchill Sit down.

Jock smiles and sits down opposite Churchill.

(*Indicating his cigar.*) Would you like one of these?

Jock Oh, well, I don't normally –

Churchill Romeo y Julieta Havanas. The finest cigars in the world. Have you ever had one?

Jock No.

Churchill Well, it's time you did then.

Churchill pushes the box towards him and Jock takes a cigar.

Now cut the end off it.

He pushes a knife towards him and Jock cuts the end off the cigar.

Then he puts it in his mouth, lights it and puffs on it.

Pretty good, huh?

Jock . . . Yes.

*He nods enthusiastically but is clearly not as taken
with them as Churchill.*
Churchill smiles.

Churchill So, what is it you wanted to discuss?

Jock Well, it's just that . . . well, over the last few days,
I've been thinking about things . . .

Churchill Oh yes.

Jock Yes, you know the war and everything, and . . .
well, I've been asking myself, am I doing enough?

He hesitates.

Churchill Enough?

Jock Yes. For the country, I mean. When so many
people are sacrificing so much. I mean, in Calais for
example . . .

Churchill looks sad for a moment.

Churchill Mm . . .

Jock So, anyway, I just wondered if you might let me . . .
join up?

Churchill is surprised.

Churchill Join up?

Jock Yes. You see, I have one brother in the Army and
one in the Navy, so I thought I'd try for the RAF . . . In
fact, I've already had contact lenses made so I can pass
the eyesight test.

Churchill Have you, indeed?

Jock Yes.

Beat.

Churchill I see.

Pause.

So you want to desert me?

Jock is taken aback.

Jock Well . . . I didn't think of it like –

Churchill Is it really so terrible working for me?

Jock No, on the contrary. I'm having the time of my life. That's what I feel so guilty about.

Churchill looks at him.

Sorry, is that a terrible thing to say?

Churchill Not if it's the truth.

Jock Well, it is. But I sometimes think there must be something wrong with me – how exciting I find it all, as the news is all so terrible and everyone else seems so full of dark looks and knitted brows, but I just can't seem to feel nearly as depressed as I ought.

Churchill Yes, well, to tell you the truth, that is exactly how I feel too.

They smile.

But to answer your question, I'm afraid the answer is no. We need you here. So you must stay in the job for which you were trained.

Jock is disappointed.

Jock Oh . . . right . . . Very good, sir.

Pause.
   Jock gets up.

Well, if it's all right, I think I'd better get some sleep.

Churchill Yes, good idea.

Jock hesitates, wondering what to do with the cigar.

You can take that with you.

Jock . . . Thank you.

He goes to the door.

Churchill And Jock?

Jock looks around.

I don't blame you for asking. That's what I'd do if I were your age.

Jock smiles.

And when the country really needs you – when the killing really begins – then I'll let you go.

Jock smiles broadly.

Jock Thank you, sir.

Churchill smiles.

Churchill Good night, Jock.

Jock Good night, sir.

Jock goes and Churchill is left alone with his cigar, whisky and revolver.
The lights fade.

EPILOGUE

Jock comes to the front of the stage and faces the audience.

Jock In the next seven days 225,000 British and 113,000 French troops were rescued from Dunkirk ready to fight another day.

Beat.

Whether it was the RAF, the Navy, the armada of little ships, the German bombs muffled by the sand, the fog, or the sacrifice at Calais, which Churchill called 'the bit of grit that saved us' . . . the miracle I, and the rest of the country, had asked for, had been granted.

Pause.

Two weeks later France capitulated . . . For a year, Britain then stood alone against Hitler.

Beat.

Then he attacked Russia . . .

Beat.

He would never again come as close to winning the war as he did between the 26th and the 28th of May 1940.

Pause.

Churchill once said –

A spot comes up on Churchill still sitting in the Cabinet room with his cigar.

Churchill History will be kind to me, for I intend to write it.

Jock smiles.

Jock And he was as good as his word. He wrote six volumes on the Second World War. But, sparing Halifax's blushes, all he said about those three days in London in May 1940 was –

Churchill Future generations may deem it noteworthy that the supreme question of whether we should fight on alone never found a place upon the War Cabinet agenda . . . We were much too busy to waste time on such academic, unreal issues.

Jock raises an eyebrow.

Pause.

Jock Chamberlain died of cancer a few months later, still unredeemed in the public mind, whilst Halifax, to his chagrin, was shipped off to America as Ambassador to Washington.

Beat.

As for me, I managed to get into the RAF just in time for D-Day, for which Churchill gave me three months' 'fighting holiday' on condition that if still alive at the end of it, I report back for duty at Number Ten.

He smiles.

Luckily, I did . . . though life was never quite so intense, frightening and momentous again.

He reflects.

But I shall give the last word to Stalin.

He thinks.

You see, some time towards the end of the war, the Prime Minister went to Moscow to see Stalin, who made a toast that night at dinner. And do you know what he said?

He looks at the audience.

He said that he could think of no other instance in history when the future of the world depended on the courage of one man.

He reflects for a moment.
 Then walks off the stage as the lights fade to a single spot on Churchill in profile as the smoke rises from his cigar.
 Then fades to black.

The End.